South Carolina Ecoregions

- Blue Ridge
- Piedmont
- Southeastern Plains
- Middle Atlantic Coastal Plain
- Southern Coastal Plain

1. Devils Fork State Park
2. Table Rock State Park
3. Caesars Head State Park
4. Jones Gap State Park
5. Goodale State Park
6. Chester State Park
7. Sesquicentennial State Park
8. Carolina Sandhills National Wildlife Refuge
9. Caw Caw Interpretive Center
10. South Carolina State Museum
11. Myrtle Beach State Park Nature Center
12. Huntington Beach State Park
13. Santee National Wildlife Refuge
14. Cape Romain National Wildlife Refuge
15. Hunting Island State Park
16. Tybee National Wildlife Refuge
17. Ernest F. Hollings Ace Basin National Wildlife Refuge
18. Savannah National Wildlife Refuge
19. Pinckney Island National Wildlife Refuge
20. Lake Warren State Park
21. Congaree National Park
22. Audubon Center & Sanctuary at Beidler Forest
23. Hamilton Branch State Recreation Area
24. Avian Conservation Center

A POCKET NATURALIST® GUIDE

SOUTH CAROLINA WILDLIFE – A Folding Pocket Guide to Familiar Animals

WATERFORD PRESS

SOUTH CAROLINA WILDLIFE

A Folding Pocket Guide to Familiar Animals

Moon Jellyfish
Aurelia aurita To 16 in. (40 cm)
Commonly washed up on beaches after storms.

Sea Nettle
Chrysaora quinquecirrha
To 10 in. (25 cm)

Atlantic Purple Sea Urchin
Arbacia punctulata
Body to 2 in. (5 cm)

Common Sea Star
Asterias forbesi
To 10 in. (25 cm)
May be tan, brown, orange or olive with orange highlights.

Eastern Oyster
Crassostrea virginica
To 10 in. (25 cm)

Lettered Olive
Oliva sayana
To 2.5 in. (6 cm)
Marks on shell resemble lettering. **South Carolina's state shell.**

Atlantic Bay Scallop
Argopecten irradians
To 3 in. (8 cm)

Lightning Whelk
Busycon contrarium
To 15 in. (38 cm)
Shell spirals to the left.

Stiff Pen Shell
Atrina rigida
To 11 in. (28 cm)

Keyhole Urchin
Mellita quinquiesperforata
To 6 in. (15 cm)
White skeletons often wash ashore.

Blue Crab
Callinectes sapidus
To 9 in. (23 cm)

Stone Crab
Menippe mercenaria
To 4.5 in. (12 cm)

Ghost Crab
Ocypode quadrata
To 2 in. (5 cm)

Horseshoe Crab
Limulus polyphemus
To 12 in. (30 cm) wide.

Fiddler Crab
Uca spp.
To 1.5 in. (4 cm)

Pipevine Swallowtail
Battus philenor
To 3.5 in. (9 cm)

Cabbage White
Pieris rapae
To 2 in. (5 cm)
One of the most common butterflies.

Eastern Tiger Swallowtail
Papilio glaucus
To 6 in. (15 cm)
South Carolina's state butterfly.

Common Sulphur
Colias philodice
To 2 in. (5 cm)

Southern Dogface
Zerene cesonia
To 2.5 in. (6 cm)
Note poodle-head pattern on forewings.

Great Purple Hairstreak
Atlides halesus
To 1.5 in. (4 cm)
Iridescent blue butterfly has two black tails on each hindwing.

Underwings

Silver-spotted Skipper
Epargyreus clarus
To 2.5 in. (6 cm)
Has a large, irregular silver patch on the underside of its hindwings. Patch is absent on the forewings.

Monarch
Danaus plexippus
To 4 in. (10 cm)
Note rows of white spots on edges of wings.

Queen
Danaus gilippus
To 3.5 in. (9 cm)

Carolina Satyr
Hermeuptychia sosybius
To 1.5 in. (4 cm)

Buckeye
Junonia coenia
To 3.5 in. (9 cm)

Mourning Cloak
Nymphalis antiopa
To 3.5 in. (9 cm)

Zebra Longwing
Heliconius charithonia
To 3.5 in. (9 cm)

Red Admiral
Vanessa atalanta
To 2.5 in. (6 cm)

Question Mark
Polygonia interrogationis To 2.5 in. (6 cm)
Silvery mark on underwings resembles a question mark.

Rainbow Trout
Oncorhynchus mykiss To 44 in. (1.1 m)
Note reddish side stripe.

Black Crappie
Pomoxis nigromaculatus
To 16 in. (40 cm)

Brown Bullhead
Ameiurus nebulosus To 20 in. (50 cm)
Brown above, white below with mottled sides.

Redbreast Sunfish
Lepomis auritus
To 11 in. (28 cm)

Channel Catfish
Ictalurus punctatus To 4 ft. (1.2 m)
Note prominent "whiskers."

Redear Sunfish
Lepomis microlophus
To 14 in. (35 cm)

Chain Pickerel
Esox niger To 31 in. (78 cm)
Has chain-like pattern on sides.

Bluegill
Lepomis macrochirus To 16 in. (40 cm)

Largemouth Bass
Micropterus salmoides To 40 in. (1 m)
Jaw joint extends beyond the eye.

Striped Bass
Morone saxatilis To 6 ft. (1.8 m)
South Carolina's state fish.

White Bass
Morone chrysops To 18 in. (45 cm)
Silvery fish has 4-7 dark side stripes.

Weakfish
Cynoscion regalis To 3 ft. (90 cm)
Back is covered with small spots.

Redfish
Sciaenops ocellatus To 5 ft. (1.5 m)
Has black spot at base of caudal fin. Also called red drum.

Southern Flounder
Paralichthys lethostigma
To 3 ft. (90 cm)

Southern Toad
Anaxyrus terrestris To 4.5 in. (11 cm)
Call is a high trill.

Bullfrog
Lithobates catesbeianus To 8 in. (20 cm)
Call is a deep-pitched – jug-o-rum.

Spring Peeper
Pseudacris crucifer
To 1.5 in. (4 cm)
Musical call is a series of short peeps.

Loggerhead
Caretta caretta To 4 ft. (1.2 m)
South Carolina's state reptile.

Yellow-Spotted Salamander
Ambystoma maculatum
To 10 in. (25 cm)
South Carolina's state amphibian.

Eastern Painted Turtle
Chrysemys picta picta
To 10 in. (25 cm)

American Alligator
Alligator mississippiensis
To 20 ft. (6 m)

Green Anole
Anolis carolinensis To 8 in. (20 cm)

Eastern Fence Lizard
Sceloporus undulatus To 8 in. (20 cm)
Has dark, zigzag bars down its back.

Copperhead
Agkistrodon contortrix To 52 in. (1.3 m)
Venomous.

Common Garter Snake
Thamnophis sirtalis sirtalis
To 4 ft. (1.2 m)
Green, brown or black snake has yellowish back stripes.

Rough Green Snake
Opheodrys aestivus To 4 ft. (1.2 m)

Black Rat Snake
Elaphe obsoleta obsoleta
To 8 ft. (2.4 m)

Red-bellied Snake
Storeria occipitomaculata
To 16 in. (40 cm)

Southern Ringneck Snake
Diadophis punctatus punctatus
To 30 in. (75 cm)

Timber Rattlesnake
Crotalus horridus
To 6 ft. (1.8 m)

Northern Water Snake
Nerodia sipedon To 4.5 ft. (1.4 m)
Note dark blotches on back.

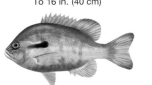

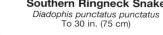

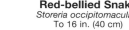

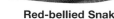
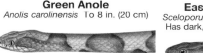

Blue-winged Teal ♂
Spatula discors To 16 in. (40 cm)

Mallard ♀ ♂
Anas platyrhynchos To 28 in. (70 cm)

Green-winged Teal ♂
Anas crecca To 16 in. (40 cm)

Bufflehead ♂
Bucephala albeola To 15 in. (38 cm)

American Wigeon ♀
Mareca americana To 23 in. (58 cm)

Wood Duck
Aix sponsa To 20 in. (50 cm)

Double-crested Cormorant
Phalacrocorax auritus To 3 ft. (90 cm)

American Oystercatcher
Haematopus palliatus To 20 in. (50 cm)

Sanderling
Calidris alba To 8 in. (20 cm)
Runs in and out with waves along shorelines.

Belted Kingfisher
Megaceryle alcyon To 14 in. (35 cm)

American Coot
Fulica americana To 16 in. (40 cm)

Cattle Egret
Bubulcus ibis To 20 in. (50 cm)
Note black bill and yellow feet.

Snowy Egret
Egretta thula To 26 in. (65 cm)
Note black bill and yellow feet.

Great Egret
Ardea alba To 38 in. (95 cm)
Note yellow bill and black feet.

Great Blue Heron
Ardea herodias To 4.5 ft. (1.4 m)

Common Gallinule
Gallinula galeata To 14 in. (35 cm)

White Ibis
Eudocimus albus To 28 in. (70 cm)
The similar glossy ibis has red-brown plumage.

Brown Pelican
Pelecanus occidentalis To 50 in. (1.3 m)

Herring Gull
Larus argentatus To 26 in. (65 cm)
Legs are pinkish.

Laughing Gull
Leucophaeus atricilla To 18 in. (45 cm)

Ring-billed Gull
Larus delawarensis To 20 in. (50 cm)
Bill has dark ring.

Black Skimmer
Rynchops niger To 20 in. (50 cm)
Feeds by skimming over water with its lower bill cutting the water's surface.

Common Nighthawk
Chordeiles minor To 10 in. (25 cm)
Often hawks for insects around street lights.

Mourning Dove
Zenaida macroura To 13 in. (33 cm)
Call is a mournful – ooah-woo-woo-woo.

Wild Turkey
Meleagris gallopavo To 4 ft. (1.2 m)
South Carolina's state game bird.

Ruby-throated Hummingbird
Archilochus colubris To 3.5 in. (9 cm)

Yellow-billed Cuckoo
Coccyzus americanus To 14 in. (35 cm)

Downy Woodpecker
Dryobates pubescens To 6 in. (15 cm)
The similar hairy woodpecker is larger and has a longer bill.

Red-headed Woodpecker
Melanerpes erythrocephalus To 10 in. (25 cm)

Yellow-shafted
Northern Flicker
Colaptes auratus To 13 in. (33 cm)

Pileated Woodpecker
Dryocopus pileatus To 17 in. (43 cm)
Note large size.

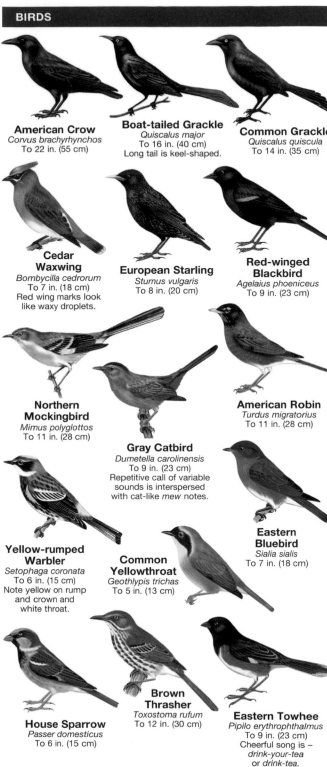

Turkey Vulture
Cathartes aura To 32 in. (80 cm)
Note red head.

Black Vulture
Coragyps atratus To 27 in. (68 cm)

Bald Eagle
Haliaeetus leucocephalus To 40 in. (1 m)

Osprey
Pandion haliaetus To 2 ft. (60 cm)

American Kestrel
Falco sparverius To 12 in. (30 cm)

Barred Owl
Strix varia To 2 ft. (60 cm)
Call is a loud – "Who-cooks-for-you? Who-cooks-or-you-all?"

Great Horned Owl
Bubo virginianus To 25 in. (63 cm)
Call is a resonant – hoo-HOO-hoooo.

Great Crested Flycatcher
Myiarchus crinitus To 9 in. (23 cm)

Eastern Kingbird
Tyrannus tyrannus To 8 in. (20 cm)
Note broad white tail band.

Purple Martin
Progne subis To 8 in. (20 cm)

Carolina Chickadee
Poecile carolinensis To 4.5 in. (11 cm)
Song is a name-saying – chickadee-dee-dee.

Brown-headed Nuthatch
Sitta pusilla To 4.5 in. (11 cm)

Barn Swallow
Hirundo rustica To 8 in. (20 cm)
Note deeply forked tail.

Tufted Titmouse
Baeolophus bicolor To 6 in. (15 cm)

Blue Jay
Cyanocitta cristata To 14 in. (35 cm)

Carolina Wren
Thryothorus ludovicianus To 6 in. (15 cm)
Note white eyebrow stripe and wing bars.
South Carolina's state bird.

American Crow
Corvus brachyrhynchos To 22 in. (55 cm)

Boat-tailed Grackle
Quiscalus major To 16 in. (40 cm)
Long tail is keel-shaped.

Common Grackle
Quiscalus quiscula To 14 in. (35 cm)

Cedar Waxwing
Bombycilla cedrorum To 7 in. (18 cm)
Red wing marks look like waxy droplets.

European Starling
Sturnus vulgaris To 8 in. (20 cm)

Red-winged Blackbird
Agelaius phoeniceus To 9 in. (23 cm)

Northern Mockingbird
Mimus polyglottos To 11 in. (28 cm)

American Robin
Turdus migratorius To 11 in. (28 cm)

Gray Catbird
Dumetella carolinensis To 9 in. (23 cm)
Repetitive call of variable sounds is interspersed with cat-like mew notes.

Yellow-rumped Warbler
Setophaga coronata To 6 in. (15 cm)
Note yellow on rump and crown and white throat.

Common Yellowthroat
Geothlypis trichas To 5 in. (13 cm)

Eastern Bluebird
Sialia sialis To 7 in. (18 cm)

House Sparrow
Passer domesticus To 6 in. (15 cm)

Brown Thrasher
Toxostoma rufum To 12 in. (30 cm)

Eastern Towhee
Pipilo erythrophthalmus To 9 in. (23 cm)
Cheerful song is – drink-your-tea or drink-tea.

Summer Tanager
Piranga rubra To 8 in. (20 cm)

Northern Cardinal
Cardinalis cardinalis To 9 in. (23 cm)

Dark-eyed Junco
Junco hyemalis To 7 in. (18 cm)

House Finch
Haemorhous mexicanus To 6 in. (15 cm)

Blue Grosbeak
Passerina caerulea To 8 in. (20 cm)

Indigo Bunting
Passerina cyanea To 6 in. (15 cm)

Virginia Opossum
Didelphis virginiana To 40 in. (1 m)
Note long fur and naked tail.

Big Brown Bat
Eptesicus fuscus To 5 in. (13 cm)

Eastern Cottontail
Sylvilagus floridanus To 18 in. (45 cm)

Eastern Chipmunk
Tamias striatus To 12 in. (30 cm)
Note white stripes on side and face.

Marsh Rabbit
Sylvilagus palustris To 18 in. (45 cm)

Norway Rat
Rattus norvegicus To 18 in. (45 cm)
Brown-to-gray rodent has a naked tail.

Eastern Gray Squirrel
Sciurus carolinensis To 20 in. (50 cm)

Fox Squirrel
Sciurus niger To 28 in. (70 cm)
Note large size and bushy tail. Largest squirrel in the US.

Nine-banded Armadillo
Dasypus novemcinctus To 32 in. (80 cm)

Common Muskrat
Ondatra zibethicus To 2 ft. (60 cm)
Aquatic rodent has a naked tail that is flattened on its sides.

Common Raccoon
Procyon lotor To 40 in. (1 m)

Striped Skunk
Mephitis mephitis To 32 in. (80 cm)

American Beaver
Castor canadensis To 4 ft. (1.2 m)

Long-tailed Weasel
Mustela frenata To 21 in. (53 cm)
Note brown feet and yellowish neck.

Mink
Neovison vison To 28 in. (70 cm)
Chin is white.

Coyote
Canis latrans To 52 in. (1.3 m)
Note bushy, black-tipped tail.

Common Gray Fox
Urocyon cinereoargenteus To 3.5 ft. (1.1 m)
Note black-tipped tail.

Black Bear
Ursus americanus To 6 ft. (1.8 m)

Bobcat
Lynx rufus To 4 ft. (1.2 m)

White-tailed Deer
Odocoileus virginianus To 7 ft. (2.1 m)
South Carolina's state animal.

Eurasian Wild Hog
Sus scrofa To 6 ft. (1.8 m)
Introduced species is descended from the Eurasian wild boar.